HOW WE USE GLOBES

Juliet Figorito

REAL LIFE readers™

Rosen Classroom™

New York

Our world is called **Earth**.

Earth is shaped like a ball.

A globe is a map of Earth.

Most maps are flat, but a globe

is shaped like a ball.

Many globes have words that tell us what we are looking at.

The words are names of places on Earth.

A globe spins around.
This makes it easy to find
different places.

A globe shows where Earth's land is.

A globe shows different **countries**.

This globe is showing North America.

The person is pointing to the United States.

The United States is a country in

North America.

A globe shows where Earth's water is.
A globe shows Earth's **oceans**, rivers, and lakes.

Earth has five oceans.

This globe is showing the Pacific Ocean.

It is Earth's largest ocean.

Globes and maps can teach us a lot about our world.

GLOBE · MAP

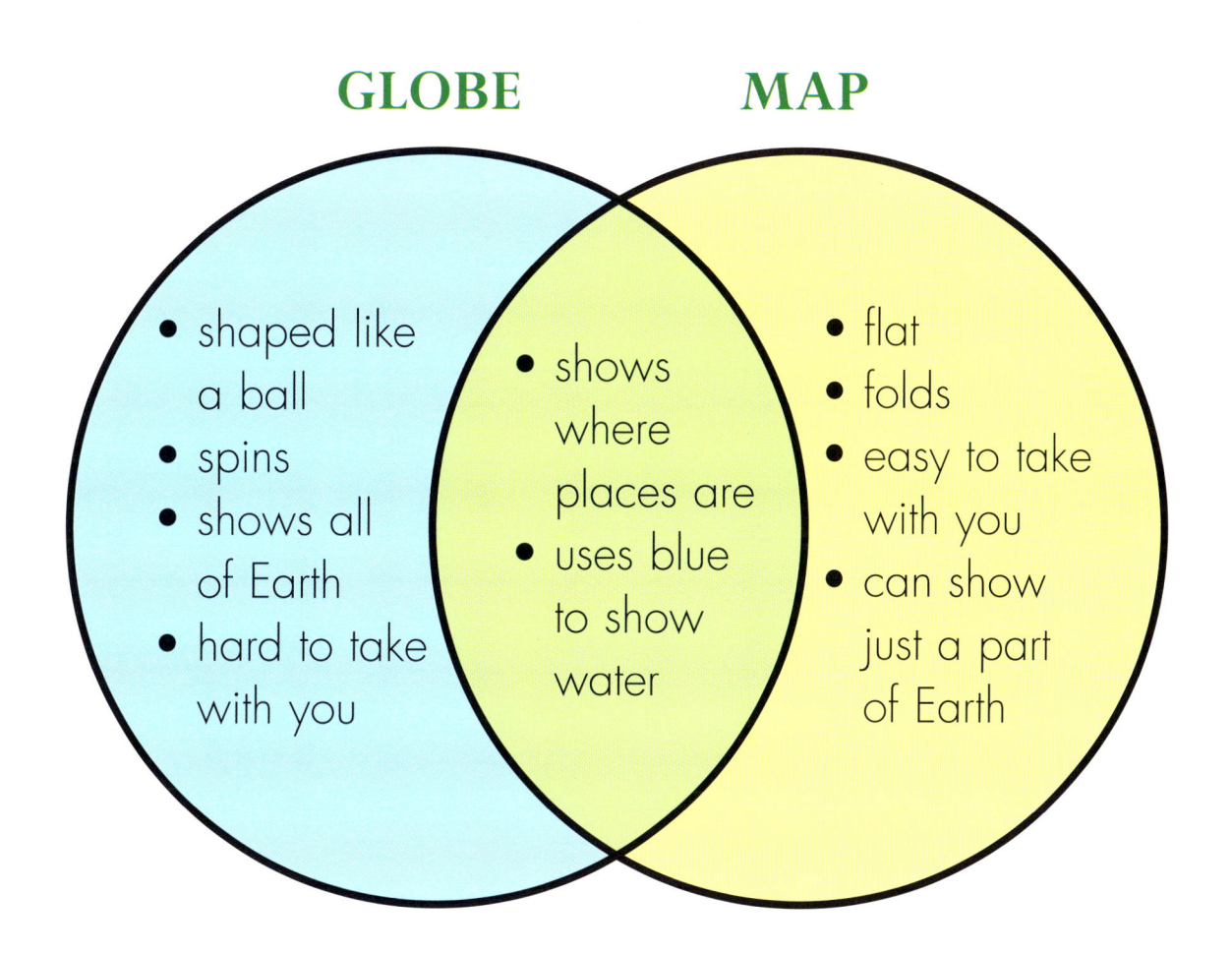

GLOBE
- shaped like a ball
- spins
- shows all of Earth
- hard to take with you

Both
- shows where places are
- uses blue to show water

MAP
- flat
- folds
- easy to take with you
- can show just a part of Earth

How are globes and maps the same?

How are they different?

GLOSSARY

country A nation of the world.

Earth The world where we live.

ocean One of the five large bodies of water on Earth.